The

DECISION

of a

LIFETIME

The DECISION *of a* LIFETIME

MARILYN MEBERG

W PUBLISHING GROUP
A Division of Thomas Nelson Publishers
Since 1798

www.wpublishinggroup.com

The Decision of a Lifetime

Published by W Publishing Group, a Division of Thomas Nelson, Inc., P.O. Box 141000, Nashville, TN 37214.

Unless otherwise indicated, Scripture quotations used in this book are from The Holy Bible, New Living Translation (NLT), copyright © 1996 by Tyndale House Publishers, Wheaton, Illinois. Used by permission.

Other Scripture references are from the following sources:

New American Standard Bible (NASB), © 1960, 1977, by the Lockman Foundation.

The Holy Bible, New International Version (NIV). Copyright © 1973, 1978, 1984, International Bible Society. Used by permission of Zondervan Bible Publishers.

The New King James Version (NKJV®), copyright 1979, 1980, 1982, Thomas Nelson, Inc., Publishers.

Library of Congress Cataloging-in-Publication Data

Meberg, Marilyn.
    The decision of a lifetime / by Marilyn Meberg.
      p. cm.
    ISBN 0-8499-4420-1 (softcover)
    1. Conversion--Christianity. I. Title.
BV4921.3.M43 2003
248.2'4--dc21   2003002246

Printed in the United States of America
04 05 06 07 08 OPM 9 8 7 6

CONTENTS

THE GREATEST QUESTION
ON THE PLANET

*L*ike a puzzle, every decision we make pops a little piece of our lives into place and establishes a pattern. For example, I decided to accept Ken Meberg's marriage proposal, and the result was a beautiful baby boy, Jeff Meberg. What if I had married Charlie Dillbean? There would never have been a Jeff—instead perhaps only a series of little Dillbeans whom I know I could not love like I love Jeff. And what about our adorable adopted daughter, Beth? If I hadn't chosen Ken as my mate, Beth would have been placed into some other couple's home, where she could not possibly have known the richness of soul we provided. (That, of course, is my biased opinion.)

And another thing: What if Ken and I had stayed in Seattle (we met at Seattle Pacific University) instead of moving to Southern California after graduation? No doubt by now I would be in the Seattle Home for Mutterers repeatedly muttering, "Where is the sun? . . . *Is* there a sun? . . . If there is a sun, why can't I ever see it?" In Southern California we became part of an incredibly stimulating community of friends and colleagues whose influence has had extraordinary impact on my life. One of those contacts led me to an invitation to join the Women of Faith speaker team. I decided to accept that invitation, and what a rewarding choice that has been.

It can be both encouraging and sobering to realize how our decisions influence our cir-cumstances and help determine the level of contentedness we will experience in life. We have all made decisions we regret, decisions that have brought us pain. But we also have made decisions that were wise and for which we are grateful. It gives us pleasure to think back on those choices and see how those wise decisions have influenced our lives in rewarding directions. It's also encouraging to recognize that wisdom is not just a commodity someone else has but that we, too, are capable of gratifying bursts of it as well.

I hope this little book will ignite a burst of wisdom for you. My intention in writing it is to inspire you to consider the greatest question on the planet. If wisdom guides your inquiry, you will then make the decision of a lifetime—the most important choice you'll ever make.

CHAPTER 1

"I GOT CHOSE"

Our son, Jeff, at the age of seven, came running into the house after what had proven to be a disturbing sandbox conversation with his four-year-old sister, Beth. "Mama," Jeff said to me in a quavering voice, "did you and Daddy get stuck with me?"

"Baby," I crooned, "of course we did not get stuck with you! What do you mean?"

Still looking troubled, Jeff ventured, "Beth said she got 'chose' . . . but you got stuck with me!"

I gathered him up, guessing then what might

have transpired in the sandbox. Jeff is our biological son, but Ken and I had adopted Beth when she was nine days old. In our efforts to make Beth's origins seem as natural as Jeff's, we had explained that God had chosen her to be our daughter, even though I had not given birth to her.

She loved that account, especially when I told her the mommy who had given birth to her loved her so much she wanted Beth to have a very special home. It never crossed our minds Beth might put an "I-got-chose, you-din't" spin on it.

I well remember my own "chose, not-chose" conflict as a fourth grader in Mrs. Boden's classroom. We had a most insensitive system of choosing team members for various competitions. During P.E., two captains were designated by Mrs. Boden. Those captains would take turns making team selections until no one remained except the most uncoordinated kid in the room. I was always chosen first because I could run faster than anyone, and except for Charlie Dillbean, I could hit a softball the farthest.

My first-to-be-"chose" experience reversed itself when we played Quicker You Figure, a math competition. In that game (straight from the pit of hell) captains were once again assigned by Mrs. Boden. The object of the game was for each child to respond to either an addition or subtraction question. Whoever yelled the correct answer first won a point for the team.

Numbers then and now cause my eyes to glaze over, my mouth to grow dry, and my brain to drift four states away. My classmates knew that. The uncoordinated kid was always chosen first in Quicker You Figure. My position on the team was the result of a process of elimination: no one left but Marilyn. Because my brain fled to Wyoming the minute the team selections began, I inevitably had to be led to the end of the team lineup, where I remained motionless and mute until recess.

No one wants to be overlooked, ignored, or discounted in any way, but I don't believe there is anyone on earth who has not felt the sting of rejection. If that rejection happens to us often enough, the inevitable assumption is that we aren't good enough, lovable enough, or smart enough to be included. All too often then we retreat, build a protective wall, and live in isolation.

An extreme example of retreat and subsequent isolation is depicted in Ralph Ellison's powerful book *Invisible Man.* The invisible man is an unnamed black man during the 1930s in search of his identity. After repeated racially based rejections as well as slanderously humiliating accusations, he retreats from society with these words:

I am an invisible man. I am invisible, understand, simply because people refuse to see me. . . . All my life I had been looking for myself and asking

everyone except myself questions which
I, and only I, could answer.

I am struck by Ellison's line "asking questions which I, and only I, could answer." There
are basic life questions we all must ask whether
or not we have been victimized to the degree
Ellison's invisible man was. Questions like: Do I
as a human being have value? Is it based on
what I do? Can what I do become increasingly
better so I ultimately earn the experience of
being included . . . being chosen?

We generally assume our value is deter-
mined by what we *do*. If I do my job well, I may
be promoted. If I do it poorly, I may be replaced
or demoted. The same mentality is true with
human relationships. If I'm pleasant, people
will probably want to be around me. When I
snarl and hiss I'll undoubtedly find myself without lunch partners. The earthly system is easily
understood by all of us. Our performance is
crucial to success as well as social acceptability.

The mind-blowing truth about the God of the universe is that He does not use the performance system. He states His evaluation of us in the Old Testament verse Deuteronomy 7:6: "Of all the people on earth, the LORD your God has chosen you to be his own special treasure." In the mind of Creator God, there is no questioning your value. You are *chosen* by Him, and if that truth alone does not melt your socks, consider this: You are also viewed as His special treasure. You don't work toward it, earn it, or struggle to become good enough. Quite simply . . . you have been "chose."

Chapter 2

Better Than a Garage Sale Masterpiece

A nursery school teacher in Cleveland Heights, Ohio, struggled with a situation famil-iar to all of us. She received a gift she couldn't stand from someone she dearly loved. The gift was a painting from her great-aunt depicting American Indians on horseback hunting buf-falo. The teacher couldn't bear to hurt her aunt's feelings by telling her that Indians chas-ing about on horseback in pursuit of buffalo was not a personally appealing subject. So she wordlessly hung the painting over her fire-place, where it stayed for years.

Ultimately, with the death of her aunt and the sense the teacher need not feel guilty about find-ing a new home for the horses and the roaming buffalo, she decided to sell it at a garage sale.

Fortunately, at the insistence of relatives and friends she consulted with art experts before holding her garage sale. The experts told her the painting was by Alfred Jacob Miller, a well-known nineteenth-century American artist, and could fetch up to $1.2 million at a Sotheby's auction.

Well . . . how about that? The teacher was in possession of a treasure! She never would have guessed the painting was a treasure or that it had great value. It seemed so ordinary . . . not especially appealing. In her mind the best place for it had been in a garage sale.

Similarly, few of us have any comprehension that we have value far greater than any master-piece to be sold at a Sotheby's art auction. Most of us assume we're closer to being garage sale material: ordinary and not especially appealing. Perhaps that's why it is so hard for us to grasp the fact that each of us is a very major masterpiece treasured by God. How do we know for sure He feels that way? The Bible says so . . . over and over again!

Why do you suppose it's so difficult to accept that divine opinion of ourselves? Why don't we just settle down and allow God to be what He wishes to be—our daily companion? As I described earlier, our society operates on a performance system. Very few of us see judges waving placards with huge tens on them to affirm we've earned the highest performance rating possible. Some participants in the Olympics have the "ten" experience, a few movies get five out of five stars from the reviewers, and several citizens get "distinguished service" awards, etc. But most people move about their lives attempting to be good citizens, good parents, good friends, blah, blah, blah, knowing that sometimes we will pull it off and sometimes we won't.

When we don't show our "best" side we hope desperately no one notices. If people do notice, we hope they have short memories.

In addition to our society system, I believe there's something else contributing to our reluctance to believe we're treasures. Quite simply, the concept is foreign to our ears. Many persons were raised with well-meaning but nonaffirming parents who simply expected their children to get A's in spelling, not stick bubblegum in some kid's hair during reading group, and wash their hands before eating. Good behavior was expected but not rewarded. Bad behavior was singled out for various levels of discipline. The most devastating would be words like, "You're always making mistakes. You never get it right. If this is the best you can do, you'll be a failure all your life." For many of us, such words of personal condemnation ring in our ears for a lifetime. It's almost as if there's a tape recorder in our minds that plays them continually and refuses to shut off.

Those who've experienced the heartbreak of divorce know very well how impossible it is to feel like a treasure when the spouse no longer wants to stay and the kids waffle about with whom they want to live. Perhaps the church, which is supposed to be a haven for the hurting, also pulls away, and one is left with the relentless tape recorder messages: *You're a failure. You'll never get it right. You aren't lovable. You never will be.*

I recently read a true story of a young girl who had never experienced love, only rejection and abandonment. She came to Covenant House in New York City on a bone-chilling cold night seeking momentary escape from the streets as well as the weather. Covenant House is a Catholic organization that offers shelter for homeless kids often caught in the web of drugs, alcohol, and prostitution.

The nun who responded to the knock on the door was not surprised at the sight of the wet, bedraggled child who stood in the doorway. That sight was tragically familiar. What was not familiar was the paint can the child clutched close to her body, attempting to shield it from the rain.

As the days passed, the sisters were pleased to note the child was eating well and sleeping well. But they also noted she was never without her paint bucket. It was placed on the floor next to her bed at night, just outside the shower when she bathed, and between her feet when she ate.

She would pull away from others to spend time alone. Then she could be heard singing to the bucket, talking to the bucket, and crying over the bucket. One day, overwhelmed with curiosity, one of the sisters asked, "Honey, what is in your bucket that is so valuable to you?"

The girl's quiet response was, "My mother."

The account the child told was heart-wrenching, even for that dear woman who was accustomed to painful stories. The child, whom I'll call Kathy, told the sister she had been thrown into a Dumpster when she was two days old. A policeman heard her cries and pulled her from the Dumpster. She was raised in a series of foster homes. Her primary motivation for living had been to one day find her mother and ask, "Why? Why did you throw me away?"

A week before Kathy came to Covenant House, she was helped in identifying and locating her mother in a New York City hospital. When Kathy walked into the hospital room she was told her mother was dying of AIDS. The anger Kathy had felt all her life suddenly melted as she looked at the dying, shriveled face of the mother she was seeing for the first time.

Kathy approached the bed and told her mother who she was and what had happened when she was two days old. In a choked whisper, Kathy heard the words, "Honey . . . I'm so sorry. I love you." Later that night, her mother died.

As Kathy concluded her story she smiled faintly and said, "The hospital gave me her cremains. That's what's in my bucket." There was a silence, and then Kathy said, "She loved me . . . she told me so."

Oddly enough, we have a common bond with Kathy. We desperately want to hear the words "I love you." Those words are like drops of water on our parched and love-starved souls.

Like Kathy, we've all probably experienced some sense of being thrown away—by divorce, by the rebellion of one of our kids, by a boss's disapproval, by a friend's rejection, by criticism from a parent . . . the list goes on.

What's the answer to this common soul devastation? *God!* Here's what He has to say to those of us who see ourselves as devalued throwaways: "I have chosen you and will not throw you away" (Isaiah 41:9). All of the Bible tells us we have been chosen, we are loved, and . . . we will never be thrown away by Him.

What are we chosen for? We've been chosen for a relationship with Him.

Why? Because we are His treasured masterpieces. A heavenly treasure is never thrown away; neither is it sold at a garage sale.

CHAPTER 3

HOW ABOUT A FEW FACTS?

*N*ot long ago I was sitting in a hotel room in Ames, Iowa, feeling mildly disgruntled. My problem was that I had made a decision the previous night based on inadequate information. As a result, I regretted my decision. Here's what happened:

As I was checking in at the hotel for our Women of Faith conference, the charming desk clerk handed me my key and then asked if I would like a fish. I stared mindlessly at him and then said, "Actually, I prefer pasta."

"OK, ma'am. Have a pleasant stay with us."

Wheeling away with my luggage, I pondered that encounter. *No one has ever attempted to take my dinner order while handing me my room key. What was that about?*

At breakfast the next morning, Luci Swindoll enthusiastically asked if I'd gotten my fish.

"What is the big deal about fish around here?" I answered. "I thought Iowa was known for corn-fed pork—not fish! Besides, Luci, I don't even like fish!"

Her response was, "Oh, you'd love this fish. Everyone who checks in can have a little goldfish in a tiny bowl to spend the night with you."

Well shoot, I thought, *I want a little goldfish to spend the night with me. So that's what the kid at the desk was talking about. Why didn't he explain the fish thing to me?* I hadn't been given the facts. I called the front desk immediately after breakfast to request my fish. I was put on a waiting list.

To what degree do facts determine *your* decisions? Frankly, I tend to be a "fly-by-the-seat-of-the-pants" type of decision maker. I like to know the facts, but sometimes there's simply too much information. Sometimes I just want to leap in there and risk it. My husband, Ken, on the other hand, was a facts man. To the degree he could, he gathered all the facts. He believed an ill-informed decision was a bad decision. (If he were still living, we would probably have gotten a fish.)

I think it is wise to be a fact gatherer and to make well-informed decisions based on those facts. But sometimes I don't make decisions that way. As a result, I tend to judge myself for being too spontaneous. The truth is, though, some experiences come into our lives whether or not we have the facts.

For instance, I found myself pregnant with our second child, Joani, one year earlier than planned. The fact was, we believed a three-year space between Jeff and his new sibling would be better for him. He would remain King Baby one year longer before his throne was usurped by another little prince or princess. I had agreed to the three-year space plan but was really thrilled at the prospect of a new baby sooner than expected. I decided rather than to have Jeff knocked off his throne we would simply have two thrones!

Joani was born July 14, 1966, in a nearly effortless delivery. Because Jeff had taken nearly eighteen hours to arrive, I assumed Joani would be a slowpoke as well. We sauntered to the hospital only to have a sudden increase in contractions while waiting to check in. I was rushed to the delivery room and barely got there in time for her world debut. She was stunningly beautiful . . . no wrinkles . . . chubby and pink. So I thought it odd that no one in the delivery room was sharing my euphoria over our new princess. I assumed seeing babies born every day had become too familiar for the medical staff to show my kind of enthusiasm. When I was told she had spina bifida, I partially understood the delivery-room mood, but I'd never heard of spina bifida. Could it really be all that bad?

It was and is. Since 1966 much progress has been made in meeting the tremendous challenges that come with spina bifida, but a number of medically ill-informed decisions were made in Joani's case. She developed spinal meningitis and as a result of that severe complication died July 29, fifteen days after she was born. We, of course, were devastated.

Several months after Joani's death, Ken and I had a conversation that proved to be extremely helpful in our mutual healing. He asked me if I would have chosen to have the Joani pregnancy if I had known she would be born with spina bifida. I knew he was not talking about abortion, but conception. Would I choose to experience the heartache of never holding her . . . never bringing her home . . . if those facts had been known to me prior to conception? Would I, based on those facts, simply decide never to have another baby after Jeff?

My heart wound was still very fresh when this conversation took place, but within minutes I knew the answer to Ken's hypothetical question. I would choose to conceive even if I knew that conception would produce a little Joani with spina bifida.

I wasn't able to fully articulate my feelings then or give the reasons why. But it was clear to me I would choose to have that baby in spite of her physical challenges. When Ken agreed, saying he felt exactly the same way, we both felt incredible relief. We were one when she was conceived. We were one in our acceptance of her brief life.

It might seem peculiar, then, that the potential of a future spina bifida birth caused us both to agree not to risk another pregnancy. Instead, a year later we adopted little Beth, who was also stunningly beautiful when she came to live with us nine days after her birth.

What I have come to realize is many of the decisions we make in a lifetime are influenced by a divine master plan. It was divinely intended that we have baby Joani. She is now a fully developed and healthy person who has life, and she lives that life in heaven. One day I will see her, know her, and even hold her. She is, and will always be. God decided that. I'm so glad He did.

Because God willed her existence does not mean Ken and I were passive bystanders in her creation. After all, the fact that I was cute, precious, and irresistible may have encouraged an earlier pregnancy than anticipated! The point is, not one of us is a passive bystander in life. Throughout our lives there are choices that must be made, and we'd be wise to gather our facts before choosing. But for those times when our knowledge of the facts does not seem to influence the circumstances in which we find ourselves, it is important to remember there is a divine master plan. The master plan that is based upon God's love for His creation provides peace in the midst of turmoil, faith in the midst of uncertainty, and joy in spite of loss. My inherent trust in the master plan is why I was so sure I'd choose the pregnancy even if I had foreknowledge about Joani's challenges. At the core of my being, I, too, knew Joani was meant to be.

It is encouraging to know we're not alone as we make our decisions in life. We have the freedom of personal choice, but we also have the promise of God's participation. Psalm 138:8 states, "The LORD will work out his plans for my life—for your faithful love, O LORD, endures forever."

We are not robots responding to divine directional switches. The way our decisions are made reflects our human uniqueness. But the existence of a divine master plan where our decisions are honored or perhaps even altered reminds us we all have the promise of a divine partnership. We'll talk about that divine master plan in the following chapter.

Chapter 4

In Spite of Mistakes

The majority of us awaken each morning with some kind of master plan for the day. It can range from the mundane necessities of dashing to the grocery store, getting the dog's teeth cleaned at the vet's, or having the tires rotated on our car, to career necessities like finishing a big project at work. Often the success of the day is based upon the completion of duties.

One of my favorite children's stories is the classic *Alexander and the Terrible, Horrible, No*

Good, Very Bad Day by Judith Viorst. Alexander knew it was going to be a terrible day when he woke up with gum in his hair. Then his best friends deserted him, dessert was left out of his lunch bag, and finally, there were lima beans for dinner and kissing on the TV. For Alexander, if there were a master plan for his day, the plan was terrible, horrible, no good, and very bad.

A number of people in San Jose, California, could identify with Alexander because they, too, are having a few no good, very bad days. For the last few months, many suburban neighborhoods there have been under siege by marauding wild pigs. The pigs look for the most green and succulent lawns and then literally chow down the entire yard.

I know I shouldn't giggle over the image of ravenous pigs devouring everything but the rocks in the side lawn, but I can't help it. Wild pigs!

Apparently what has happened is that the property, which wildlife officials say was staked out long ago for the pigs, has gradually been encroached upon by new housing developments. So I guess it makes sense, at least to the pigs: If you're living on their land, they'll eat your yard. (I still think that's funny . . . but, of course, I'm not living on pig land. Actually, I live on an enormous anthill. I don't think the ants are any happier about my presence here in Palm Desert than the pigs are with the residents in San Jose.)

In spite of our best-laid plans, we all experience being broadsided by the unexpected and the unwanted. We, too, may conclude we're having a terrible, horrible, very bad day, which for many of us may last longer than a day. To what degree does the divine master plan figure into our experiences? In fact, what is a divine master plan? Can I blame it for my terrible, horrible experience?

A verse in the Old Testament, Jeremiah 29:11, states, "'I know the plans I have for you,' says the LORD. 'They are plans for good and not for disaster, to give you a future and a hope.'" This verse clearly states that God does, indeed, have a plan for each of us. We are not creatures wandering haphazardly from point A to point B. The verse also clearly states that the plan is designed to give us a future and a hope and not terrible, horrible experiences. The degree to which we can mess up the divine master plan with poor choices or disobedience is a matter of some debate. But I do know this about the divine master plan: God created the plan to show His *love* for us, not his judgment of our mistakes. His plan offers forgiveness when we need it, encouragement when we feel weak, and clarity when we don't see clearly. Let me give you an example of a plan designed to give a future and a hope.

When Ken and I adopted Beth we frequently forgot she was adopted because she was so fully integrated into our family. We were aware, however, it would be normal for her to have questions about her origins as she grew older. As we anticipated, in her junior year of college she became interested in finding her birth parents. Beth wanted to be sure Ken and I would be OK with that. We encouraged her, although it gave us both a knot in our stomachs.

Shortly after Beth began her search, she found her birth parents in Illinois. She learned that Sherry, her biological mother, as a young teenager had come to California to have her baby in secret. After Beth was born, Sherry returned to the Midwest to begin her senior year of high school. Neither she nor the biological father, Steve, wanted to give up their baby. They wanted to marry and establish a home for their child. But instead they yielded to parental pressure, and Beth was "put up for adoption."

Steve and Sherry married shortly after high school. They had three more children. During that time Steve went to college and seminary and then entered the ministry.

The years after Beth's adoption did not heal the hole in the soul both Sherry and Steve experienced from giving up their baby. Each secretly prayed that one day they might meet that "baby," but neither anticipated it would ever happen. After all, they reasoned, there are always consequences to wrongdoing. They were suffering the consequences, and that was a fact each of them felt must be accepted. You can imagine their stunned euphoria, then, when they received that first phone call from a young woman stating, "My name is Beth, and I think you are my birth parents."

Steve is currently the pastor of a thriving, vibrant church in Marion, Ohio. Sherry and Steve are warm, loving people who want with all their hearts to help people and serve God. They are doing both.

Beth met Steve and Sherry as well as her brother Eric, and her sisters Amy and Laura a few weeks after that initial phone call. Since the "kids" had no idea there was another sister out there, there was no small amount of drama when they all met. And there was no small amount of drama when, weeks later, Steve introduced Beth to a stunned and unsuspecting Sunday morning congregation of his church as the love child of his youth whom he and Sherry had never dared to hope they could know.

What adds even more drama to this story is that Beth is now living in Marion, Ohio, three blocks from Sherry and Steve, and is an active member of Steve's church. After Beth's painful divorce last year, I longed for my grandsons, Alec and Ian, to have a stable, loving environment. They lived some distance from me, and my travel schedule with Women of Faith kept me from being as available to Beth and the boys as I would have liked. Both Sherry and Steve come from large families; all their siblings are married, have bunches of children, and live in close proximity.

Can you imagine what it must feel like for Sherry and Steve to have had a baby out of wedlock, become convinced God could not possibly use them because of their mistakes, and now to not only have Beth living in their neighborhood but to also be able to daily experience their grandchildren born of the daughter they never expected to meet? You have to admit, that is an amazing plan!

What does this story say about God's divine master plan? As I said earlier, His plan is designed to show His love for us and not His judgment. His plan offers forgiveness when we need it, encouragement when we feel weak, and clarity when we don't see clearly.

If you've ever thought you have blown it too badly for God to love you, forgive you, or make anything out of your life, remember: Not only are you a divine treasure, you are one for whom God has a plan—a plan that will give you a future and a hope.

CHAPTER 5

WHAT DOES GOD LOOK LIKE?

$\mathcal{D}$id you know there is an old law still on the books in Lexington, Kentucky, making it illegal to carry an ice-cream cone in one's back pocket?

Don't you wonder what happened to make back-pocket ice cream so offensive it was necessary to create a law against it? Did some absent-minded person sit on an expensive public chair, smearing it with peanut butter brickle laced with chocolate chips? Imagine the negative self-talk of the cone owner as she anguished over why she couldn't remember to keep the ice cream out of her back pocket in the first place.

I giggled over that law because I love anything quirky and off-the-wall. I'm especially amazed by the quirky, off-the-wall ideas people have about God. Those ideas don't always make me giggle. Just as I wonder what was behind the ice-cream law, I often wonder what's behind people's ideas about God.

I've talked to many people who sincerely believe God is whoever you want Him to be. They believe He can be an ill-defined "higher power"; He can be nature, the presence of which produces peace and harmony, especially as you hug a tree; He can even reside within an animal. (I know a dog breeder who is quite sure God is probably a golden retriever simply because they're big, easygoing dogs that love unconditionally. She didn't say if she pictures him observing us from the apex of the world with a Milkbone in his mouth.)

I was flying home from Philadelphia a few

weeks ago and gradually became aware of my seat partner's shoulder leaning into mine. There was plenty of space available between us, so I wondered why he needed to lean. I glanced at him; he returned my glance and said, "I can't read your writing."

I found his boldness amusing. "Why are you trying to read my writing?"

"Because I can occasionally make out the word *God*, and I'm curious to know what you're saying about Him."

"Are you interested in God?"

"I have ideas about Him."

Oddly enough, I didn't find this man intrusive. In fact, I liked him. He told me his name was Ed and that he sees God as a gambler. Finding myself fully engaged, I asked, "Does He do the slots, or does He do the big stuff?"

"No, He does the big stuff, but His big stuff is us. He created everything, and having tossed it all into space, He simply walked away to gamble on something else."

My heart began to sink. "You don't think God is personal? That He knows you, sees you, and loves you?"

"Not a chance. We blew it; people cheat each other and kill each other down here. It was a bad bet for Him. So He's gone off somewhere to try a different hand. Maybe the next one will be lucky!"

I asked Ed if he had any way of proving his point of view, or was he content to just create a god that fit his own assumptions? He winked at me and said when he had time he was thinking of writing a new bible. Then he added, taking a quick swig of his wine, that Jesus could not possibly be the Son of God as He claimed because He "got Himself killed." Then he added, "And that was too bad, because a person who could change water into wine would be a welcome addition to any community."

These various speculations about God, off-beat and quirky as they might be, reflect not only our tendency to create God in our own image but our overall curiosity about Him as well. Einstein said he wanted to know how God created the world. "I want to know His thoughts," he said. I believe all thinking persons share Einstein's curiosity. For that reason, it is crucial to do a thorough study of God before deciding He's a gambler or anything else that comes to our imagination.

The Bible tells us who God is and also much of what He thinks. I realize some of you reading this may be skeptics who don't believe the Bible. As my seat partner, Ed, said to me, "You can't prove your point by using a book I don't buy into." That's a fair response. The reality is, I can't prove the Bible to be true. There are, however, many convincing reasons to believe it to be true. To cite a few, Is it not interesting that this Book has inspired the highest level of moral living known to humankind? And isn't it also interesting that this Book speaks of a Christ who is admired and quoted even by skeptics? Another fact about the Bible that gives it credibility is that it is made up of sixty-six books that evolved over a period of fifteen centuries. It was written in three different languages by forty different human authors ranging from kings to fishermen. All those authors with centuries between their writings are in total agreement as they describe who God is and what His purpose is. They didn't have the luxury of checking each other's stories to make sure they were writing the same thing.

How does one account for that total unity of theme and message? Quite simply, it's because *God wrote the Book!* The Bible says, "All Scripture is inspired by God" (2 Timothy 3:16), and "It was the Holy Spirit who moved the prophets to speak from God" (2 Peter 1:21).

God has a message He wants His people to hear, so He stated it over and over through different biblical writers down through the centuries. That message has never changed: God loves His people and wants a personal relationship with them.

So, then, however you view the Bible, may

I encourage you to ponder the following biblical fact sheet about God. You will at least have the satisfaction of becoming somewhat knowledgeable about a Book that's been on the bestseller list for centuries and a God who has been around even longer. You've got nothing to lose and, in my view, everything to gain.

1. God was before everything everywhere.

"He is before all things" (Colossians 1:17 NIV).

"Before the mountains were created, before you made the earth and the world, you are God, without beginning or end." (Psalm 90:2).

2. God is the Creator of all things.

"By the word of the LORD were the heavens made, their starry host by the breath of his mouth" (Psalm 33:6 NIV).

"It is I who made the earth and created mankind upon it" (Isaiah 45:12 NIV).

"We are the clay, and you are the potter. We are all formed by your hand" (Isaiah 64:8).

"In his hand is the life of every creature and the breath of all mankind." (Job 12:10 NIV).

3. God's nature is love.

"The LORD is faithful to all his promises and loving toward all he has made" (Psalm 145:13 NIV).

"For the LORD is good and his love endures forever; his faithfulness continues through all generations" (Psalm 100:5 NIV).

"For great is your love, reaching to the heavens; your faithfulness reaches to the skies" (Psalm 57:10 NIV).

If we choose to believe that God has always been, that He is the Creator of all that is, and that His nature is love, we can stop making up our own versions of God. But we can't stop here in our formulations because there is more we need to know about Him. It is astounding to realize that two thousand years ago, in accordance with the divine master plan, God sent His

Son Jesus to this earth! This world-altering event changed the assumptions and images of God forever.

Jesus said, "He who has seen Me has seen the Father; how do you say, 'Show us the Father'?" (John 14:9 NASB). He also said, "I and My Father are one" (John 10:30 NKJV). Jesus literally became the face of God as He reflected the exquisite tenderness and compassion of God.

"And wherever he went, he healed people of every sort of disease and illness. He felt great pity for the crowds that came, because their problems were so great and they didn't know where to go for help. They were like sheep without a shepherd" (Matthew 9:35–36). Jesus' compassion moved Him to tell people the story of God's love. God's love for His people moved Him to send a Shepherd.

It is interesting how the comparison of Jesus with a shepherd and his sheep weaves its way throughout the pages of the Bible. The job of a shepherd was to protect his sheep even if it meant dying to save them. Jesus became the ultimate Shepherd. But now we come to a hard truth: It would be more appealing to us if Jesus had just continued walking the dusty roads of the Middle East, loving and helping people wherever He went. But the same compassion that moved Him to the people also moved Him to the cross. The Shepherd needed to die for us, His sheep, in order that the sheep might be saved. Saved from what? It's a condition called sin. Matthew 1:21 (NASB) tells us, "It is He who will save His people from their sins."

In the next chapter we'll talk about the unpopular and sometimes controversial subject of sin. But do know this: The problem of sin has a powerfully positive solution.

CHAPTER 6

IS IT A DONE DEAL?

*H*ow do you feel about the concept of sin? Do you find it to be slightly offensive, old-fashioned, or downright insulting? Most of us have a negative opinion of sin. Yet the Bible says we're full of it.

People who pride themselves on being sensitive family members, good citizens, or even conscientious church members often bristle at the biblical assertion that we are all sinners. The "bristlers" might agree that many people choose sin over goodness, but they believe such behavior comes as a result of choice, not as the result of promptings from an inner condition. The "bristlers" would deny they share a sin nature with everyone else on the planet. But the Bible says:

"If we claim to be without sin, we deceive ourselves and the truth is not in us" (1 John 1:8 NIV).

"There is not a righteous man on earth who does what is right and never sins" (Ecclesiastes 7:20 NIV).

I've often wondered if those persons who find it difficult to believe in an inborn sin nature ever had children. Ken and I never spent a single moment with either of our children coaching them in how to be selfish, dishonest, or disobedient, but those behaviors surfaced early in life with alarming frequency and ease. Instead we spent hours coaching them about how to share, show respect, follow the rules, and be truthful. Those darling little children were born in sin, and I might add, so were their parents.

The reason it is so important to understand the sin issue is that sin keeps us from having a relationship with God. This entire booklet has stressed how God wants a relationship with His creation. There is, however, a major challenge in achieving that goal: sin. Quite simply, sin separates us from God. Not only are we separated from Him, Romans 6:23 says "the wages of sin is death." Well, that's depressing! Mercy!

But hang on . . . here's what God did to remove the sin separation as well as the death sentence. Remember we are considered a treasure by Him. It is not His choice to throw us away, so He devised a master plan designed to eliminate the sin problem. Let's do another fact sheet in an effort to understand the plan. You might want to get a cup of something while you leisurely consider these facts.

1. God loves us.

"For God so loved the world that he gave his only Son, so that everyone who believes in him will not perish but have eternal life. God did not send his Son into the world to condemn it, but to save it" (John 3:16–17).

Why did the world need to be saved? With Adam and Eve's choice to disobey God in the Garden of Eden, sin entered the world. From that moment on, we have needed a Savior. Jesus, the Son of God, was willing to pay the penalty for our sin, which is death.

2. Jesus died in our place.

"When we were utterly helpless, Christ came at just the right time and died for us sinners" (Romans 5:6).

Remember, the penalty for sin is separation from God and eternal death. Jesus saved us from paying that penalty.

The astounding fact is Jesus did not remain dead. "God raised him from the dead, and for many days he was seen by those who had traveled with him from Galilee to Jerusalem" (Acts 13:30–31 NIV).

3. Jesus is the only way for us to have a relationship with God.

"Jesus told him, 'I am the way, the truth, and the life. No one can come to the Father except through me'" (John 14:6).

So now what?

4. We believe and receive Jesus.

"As many as received Him, to them He gave the right to become children of God, to those who believe in his name" (John 1:12 NKJV).

If we believe God is who He says He is (the loving Creator of all that is), if we believe Jesus is who He says He is (the Son of God who by His death paid the price for our sin), we have fulfilled the first requirement for a God relationship. We believe.

Perhaps a more difficult element here is knowing what it means to *receive*. There is a huge difference between believing and receiving. Receiving requires an action. For example, we can believe with all sincerity that the couch we're sitting on is on fire. We may not know how the fire started, but the reality is, the couch is burning. What do we do with that belief? We act! If we don't move off the couch, we'll burn our britches. In the same way, receiving Jesus as Savior requires an action.

What kind of action is necessary? (For this one you can stay on the couch.) To answer that question we go back to our original subject for this chapter: sin. We must confess our sin to the Jesus who died for that sin:

"Finally, I confessed all my sins to you and stopped trying to hide them. I said to myself, 'I will confess my rebellion to the LORD.' And you forgave me! All my guilt is gone" (Psalm 32:5).

What an incredible master plan! We confess the sin that's been bothering us for years. He hears our confession, forgives our sin, and the guilt is gone. Amazing!

There's another mind-boggling element in this divine master plan. Did you notice, tucked into the middle of John 1:12, the words "He gave the right to become children of God" (NKJV)? Hold those words a second and now read these: "You should behave . . . like God's very own children, adopted into His family—calling him 'Father, dear Father'" (Romans 8:15).

Do you realize what those words mean? You, dear one, were up for adoption, and God the Father chose you to be in His family. God the Father *chose* you to be His child. He even chose you to receive, as a family member, an inheritance: "For his Holy Spirit speaks to us deep in our hearts and tells us that we are God's children. And since we are his children, we will share his treasures—for everything God gives to His Son, Christ, is ours, too" (Romans 8:16–17).

What a sweet truth to realize that you are a chosen, deeply valued treasure to the God of the universe. He wants to adopt you! But unlike most adoptions, you have a choice in deciding whether you want to be adopted. At the beginning of this booklet I invited you to consider an answer to the most important question on the planet. I didn't ask it then, but I'll ask it now: How are you going to respond to God's offer of love, salvation, and personal adoption?

Because God respects personal choice, you are not pressured by Him to become a family member. You've considered the facts of who God is, what Jesus did for you, and how deeply you are loved. You've heard that God will not throw you away. You, however, can decide to throw *Him* away. You, and you alone, make that decision.

Let's assume wisdom guides your choice and you decide you want to be adopted. What do you do? What do you say? How do you close the deal? Let me suggest you simply tell the Father, through Jesus, you want to be in the family. Tell Him you agree to the terms of adoption: confession of sin and then believing in and receiving Jesus as

Savior. If you wish, you could use the following words to express yourself to Him:

> Lord Jesus, I want to be adopted into the family of God. Thank You for choosing me. Thank You, Jesus, for dying for all my sin. I believe in You, and I receive You as my Savior. I ask You to come into my life this very minute. Forgive me for the sin that has separated me from You. Thank You for promising to stay with me forever and never throwing me away. Amen.

If this prayer expresses the desire of your heart and you have agreed to the terms for your adoption, you, dear one, have just made the decision of a lifetime!

IT'S FOR KEEPS

*N*ow that you have made the decision of a lifetime, know that God will never back out of His agreement with you. Jesus will never decide you had more sin than He could die for. You will never lose your status as a treasure.

There will, however, be times when you'll wonder why God holds you in such tender regard. You'll wonder why Jesus was willing to die so that you might live. But while you're wondering, remember this: His love for you is a fact you can't change; it comes with a family membership that will never expire. Just accept it, Sweetheart . . . you got *chose!*

A Word from
Women of Faith®

*T*he moment you make this decision to begin a personal relationship with God, through His Son, Jesus Christ, He comes into your life and, as He says in Hebrews 13: 5, "I will never leave you or forsake you." You can be confident of this, even if your feelings sometimes tell you otherwise. Do not depend on feelings. Our feelings come and go, but the Bible assures us of our relationship with God, and we can be secure in that fact.

If you made this decision, we'd love to hear from you. Please write us at:

Decisions—Women of Faith
820 W. Spring Creek Parkway
Suite 100
Plano, TX 75023

Or contact us on the web site www.womenoffaith.com. We have some information we'd like to send you right away to help you grow.

We also encourage you to register the date of your decision, as a reminder to yourself that on this day, you became a child of God. He chose you. And, on this date, you've chosen to respond.

About the Author

Marilyn Meberg is an extraordinary storyteller who shares the gospel through her hilarious tales and heart-touching stories. The author of *The Zippered Heart, Choosing the Amusing,* and *I'd Rather Be Laughing,* Marilyn holds a master's degree in English and for ten years taught at Biola University. Later she earned a master's degree in counseling psychology and launched a second career focused on helping people with hurting souls. A vibrant speaker with the phenomenally popular Women of Faith® conference tour since its beginnings in 1996, Marilyn resides in Palm Desert, California.